PARTNERING WITH THE UNIVERSE

TAP INTO THE POWER THAT IS ALREADY WITHIN YOU

BY
SUSAN CAROLINE, Ph.D

PARNERING WITH THE UNIVERSE:
TAP INTO THE POWER THAT IS
ALREADY WITHIN YOU.

By Dr. Susan Caroline

Copyright ©2021

This book is licensed soley for your personal enjoyment only. It may not be re-sold. If you would like to share this book with another person, please purchase them an additional copy.
All rights reserved. This book is protected under the copyright laws of the United States of America. This book may not be copied or reprinted for commercial gain or profit. The use of short quotations or occasional page copying for personal or group study is permitted.

www.themysticheart.com

DEDICATION

To the love of my life,

My Dearest David,

and my three beautiful children,

Ashley, Judah and Malachi.

Thank you for being my greatest treasures!

And to all who feel drawn to partner with the unseen forces that surround them. May you truly know that the power to transform your life has always been within you.

Authors Note:

I do not claim this book to be a polished work. Rather, it is simple and unedited from my heart to yours. My prayer is that you would catch the spirit of love and simplicity in which it was written and be blessed by it.

CONTENTS

Introduction	7
The Promise of the Present Moment	47
How to Fly High in Life	65
How to Hear The Source Speak	85
How to Know If What You are Listening to is Harmful or Helpful	97
How to Notice when you are in Partnership with the Universe	107
Following Your Intuition	115
Perfect Planning	127
Your Mind Space	139
Infinite Possibilities	155

INTRODUCTION

Hello there dear reader. I am so excited to share some fascinating and inspiring tips on allowing the Presence, the Infinite Intelligence behind this created world we live in, to show up and be present in YOUR life. That's right, you read it correctly. The Master Mind behind this created Universe wants to show up in YOUR everyday, ordinary life. How do I know this? Because that Power continually shows up in mine, and that Presence is no respecter of persons. What God and the Universe will do for one, they will do for all!

Now when I talk about this Power showing up in your life, I am not talking metaphorically. Each day I believe that the Infinite Intelligence that created this world, wants to show up in our lives, and does. We just need to have the eyes to see. We need to become aware of what is going on in THIS PRESENT MOMENT. I am not talking about fairies, angels or strange supernatural experiences like gold dust materializing out of thin air, or other metaphysical phenomenon. No! I'm talking about direct experiences that may look extremely ordinary from an outside point of view, but let me assure you that they are anything but ordinary! You just need to open the eyes of your heart to see what is really going on!

God and the Universe are always ready, willing and able to be part of our lives. We just need to get out of the way, and allow ourselves to be open to that divine guidance and help. Trust me, life will be so much more exciting and fulfilling when we do! Imagine being able to tap into the Infinite Wisdom that keeps the planets orbiting and the stars shining, any time you desire and being able to get guidance as to what to do with your life! How could we turn away from such a great offer?

This is not some weird, hocus-pocus sort of existence. No! This is learning to tap into the place where the true you, intersects with the Presence of the Divine. I like to call this place Your Other Self.

We each have a body, and we have been

given a mind to help navigate around planet earth, but the true you, the spiritual part of you, or metaphysical part of you, is who you truly are and who you will always be. That is the part that is connected to God, the Infinite One that is the Master Mind behind the created world.

Divine Mind and the Universe

Throughout this book, I will refer to that Master Mind as either Divine Mind, Infinite Intelligence, Creator, or God. I understand that many people these days refer to God as 'the Universe.' However, in this book we will be using the term 'the Universe' in regards to the actual physical universe that we live in.

This Universe is not just immovable solid matter. Far from it! Quantum physics has shown us that this Universe is not static. It is a forever moving mass of energy. From the trees, animals, food, furniture, buildings that you see, to the clothes you wear...everything is actually energy, including you! You are energy, and the Source of that energy resides within you as the Presence of God or the Divine Mind within.

When you allow the energetic, non-physical (metaphysical) part of you to interact with the Presence of God within you, that's when the magic happens. Your universe will never be the same, because the universe is alive and active, and responds to the Presence within you. Jesus Christ demonstrated how created reality could bend to the Presence within. He superseded natural law by commanding storms, walking on water, multiplying food, raising dead people, and then turned around and made the astounding claim that others would be able to do the same thing!

He knew that inside each of us was a secret Kingdom. A place of incredible power and wholeness (holiness) where the Presence of the Infinite dwells. When you allow yourself to tap into that Presence, that Presence knows how to partner with the created world of energy, to bring about extraordinary effects in your life.

Just like the air that you breathe, the very

Presence of the Infinite is always there. You don't have to be concerned that there isn't enough air for you. You just expect it to sustain you and fill your lungs with life giving oxygen! It's the same with the Presence that permeates every molecule of the created world. It is the energy that runs throughout the entire Universe. Invisible, uncreated, intelligent energy. This Intelligence is always there, always has been there, you just haven't become conscious of that Presence that is always there to guide you. Until now.

When you become conscious of this Divine Presence, the Presence of God, that is when life starts to become truly exciting. Rather than facing problems by yourself, you now have a wonderful counselor, an advisor to help you solve life's puzzles. Before, when you didn't know what to do, you felt you were on your own, or so you thought. Now you can turn within and go to the Most High, the Divine Mind and Heart of the Universe to help you figure out what is the best course of action.

I'm sure we have all experienced times in the past when we decided to follow our intuition rather than just our head, and things worked out well...almost magically! I myself have followed the advice of this amazing Presence and met new and fabulous people, landed jobs that weren't advertised, and even met the love of my life!

As I stated before, God and the Universe work together in tandem to help you live your best life. My intention is that as you read these words, the eyes of your heart will be opened to see more and more how the Divine is *already* operating in your life. As you might have heard, what you focus on expands. The more you start paying attention and focusing in on all the ways that God is *already* operating in your life, the more you start allowing and trusting that Presence to guide and lead you in every area when you start to see all the positive results.

You see, each one of us is made in the very image of God. The Divine Presence behind this created world, the animating force lives inside of you, and wants to express life, love and freedom through you and in you! Many are awakening to the fact that they are more than just a body and a mind...there is a consciousness behind their thoughts. The Watcher. The Thinker. The Awareness. Your Other Self. When you start allowing that Self to guide you, life will become the adventure that you know you were born to live!

I'm sure every one of us have experienced synchronicities and events that we just can't explain. Whether you believe that there is a Higher Consciousness behind this physical world or not, we have all at some point in our lives experienced things that seem right out of *The Twilight Zone*.

For example, I can remember being at a very crowded event and my husband pointed out that the man walking in front of us looked like a guy we knew who we hadn't seen for many years, I'll call him Mike. At the EXACT moment as he was saying these words, my husband's phone buzzed. He looked down and saw that he had just received a Facebook friend request, from none other than Mike...the Mike that we thought the guy walking in front of us looked like! The Mike that we hadn't seen in God knows how long! That's just one example!

I'm sure each one of us have had strange things happen to us that are beyond just mere coincidence. Take a moment to reflect on your life, and I think you will be able to bring to mind at least one or two events when you had things happen that made you think that maybe there is something more going on here behind the scenes than what meets the eye!

If you look back over the past five or ten years, and think about the string of events that have brought you to where you are now, just think what would happen if you had *actively* partnered with the Presence within you. Think of all the good things that *have* happened! That Infinite Intelligence that made you and knows all about you wants to help you become the greatest version of yourself! Where do you envision yourself to be if you had access to such wisdom and consulted with that Wisdom in regard to your life?

I'm here to tell you that you do have access to that wisdom. That wisdom can only be accessed in one place, and one place only. Do you want to know where that place is? That place is in the PRESENT MOMENT!

You see, each one of us are called to co-create with God and the Universe. We don't have to figure out how we are going to get from A to B. If you want to amass a million dollars, you might not know the whole strategy. However, most of us can amass one dollar, and then another and another. Just like a fortune is created one dollar at a time, it's the same with our life. Our life is created one moment at a time.

For years I wanted to write a book, but the task seemed daunting. It put me off from ever starting. However, I realized I only had two choices. I could let fear freeze me from ever taking action, or I could begin, and trust my Other Self, that part of me that is connected with the Most High to help me one word, one sentence, one chapter at a time.

It's the same for each one of us. Each of us were put here with dreams in our heart that seem impossible, so we never even start! I'm telling you to stop looking at the big picture, and instead focus in on THIS PRESENT MOMENT!

There is no way that you could possibly foresee all the events that brought you to this very moment in time, and in the same way, you can't foresee all the events that are yet to happen in the future. Let me give you another example from my own life.

Through a series of events, I found myself living in Las Vegas in my late teens/early twenties. Coming from England with my parents, I was only supposed to be in the United States for nine months to a year, as I was on a temporary visa. Unbeknown to me, a man that I didn't know at the time, was sent from England shortly after I arrived in the States, to be stationed at Nellis Air Force Base. Las Vegas is a large city, and the Air Force base was a clear half hour drive from where I lived.

He arrived in Las Vegas after going through a breakup with an American girl in England. He had thought he had heard intuitively that his future wife would be in England, so he was stunned when things didn't end up working out with the girl he had dated while he was stationed there.

When he arrived in Las Vegas from England, he went to purchase new uniforms. The clerk who was working at the store, was wearing an unusual pin. When he asked about it, she invited him to a college group, which happened to be the one that I attended on the other side of Las Vegas. We ended up meeting, and the rest is history! We celebrate our 30 year anniversary next year. His wife (me) was English, and had been in England almost for the entire two years he was there! We just didn't meet there! There is no way that either one of us could have coordinated our meeting.

It's the same with you my friend! There are people yet for you to meet, exciting adventures and events that are still on the horizon. There is no way that you will be able to orchestrate them yourself. That's where Infinite Intelligence comes in! That's where you can see your partnership with the Universe come into play!

If the layers of the unseen realm were stripped back, we would see countless times where we ignored the prompting of the spirit. I'm sure right now, you can look back and think of a time when you ignored a prompting, only to regret it. We walk away from situations saying to ourselves, "I just knew I shouldn't have done that!" or whatever the case may be.

I believe that if we connect with the Divine Mind like Jesus Christ did, we will be able to live out the best plan for our lives. Stop looking to society to tell you what living your best life means for you! Who says a large home, or an expensive car is what would make you truly happy? Start turning inside and allow the dreams that the Universe has planted in *your mind* to come to light. It's only by living *those* dreams that you will experience "heaven on earth." Our limited human understanding is always changing. We are continually being sold by clever marketers and the media what we should like/wear/eat/buy/live in. No more! Instead allow the Presence of the Divine within you to partner with you, and lead you into your best life! The more you are able to see with the eyes of your heart what the Source of all has for you, the more fulfilled you will be!

Christ said to his early followers that we would not only be able to do the same things that he was doing, but those who followed his example would be able to do even *greater* things. That is coming from someone who walked on water, raised the dead, multiplied food that fed thousands of people, and healed many different types of sickness and diseases. Jesus recognized that he could do nothing by himself. However, he realized that he was one with the One Mind behind all things, which he lovingly called Father. One description of father means, "to come forth from." We each have come forth from one Source, and when we allow ourselves to be partnered with the Infinite, Creative Intelligent energy behind this world, we too can manifest amazing things. In fact, even the Bible talks about all creation groaning and longing for the manifestation of God's sons/daughters to be revealed. That's us! All of us.

Christ talked about each one of us becoming

like children. This does not in any way imply that we should be childish. What is meant, is that we should have full confidence and trust in the Universal Presence. When you tell a child that something is going to happen, they believe you. They have not become skeptics yet! It's the same with us. We need to know that the Divine Mind brought us into this world, and if we consult with that Mind, we will know the best course of action to take no matter what situation we might find ourselves in.

We are not orphans. We have access to Infinite Intelligence, the same 'Father" or Source that Jesus talked about. When I say this, I am not suggesting that this Divine Mind or Infinite Intelligence is a man in the sky or a Zeus like God. Jesus himself described the Source of all as Spirit. A pure consciousness that is love. We come from that place to this planet to rediscover our connection with the Divine, and know that we are never truly alone. We can partner with this incredible Intelligence that loves us deeply and is resident within us.

Imagine being born into a family of absolute privilege and wealth. Imagine being born into royalty, with anything you could possibly want or need being at your fingertips. All you have to do is ask. Your 'Father' the originating Source of where you come from is in your DNA. That energy, that life, is flowing through your veins. No matter if you deny that with your conscious mind, it still holds true. That DNA is the very fiber of who you are. It's your consciousness that decides whether to embrace that or not. You don't have to 'do' anything to be part of that privilege, because you were gifted it at birth. However, if you don't appropriate it, none of the benefits will be of any value to you.

You have been given a choice to either stay 'unconscious' and just let yourself be led along by your ego, your human persona and outside forces. Or, you can partner with the Universe, the One-Song, and allow your life to be orchestrated by the Master Mind that can see the whole symphony of your life, and not miss a note! The choice my friends, is yours!

What Shows Up On The Outside Is What Is Going On Inside

Living in Florida, we are fortunate to have many fruit trees on our property. Mangos, starfruit and oranges grow in abundance. For those not familiar with the different types of trees and their foliage, the fruit that they produce tells you for sure what type of tree they are. My mango tree is never going to produce bananas, and my starfruit tree is never going to produce avocados.

It's the same thing in our lives. If we want to know what we have been planting in our minds, we need look no further than the type of 'fruit' that is showing up in our lives. I could wish all I want that my starfruit tree would produce avocados. I could meditate for hours, do affirmation after affirmation, declare that it will in fact produce avocados, but guess what? It's never going to produce avocados. It will always produce starfruit.

If I want something different, then I am going to have to *do* something different. I'm going to have to go out and purchase an avocado tree, dig a hole, and plant it, and then continue to water and fertilize it. That, my friends, is the only way that I'm going to get the avocados I want. I am going to have to actually take action!

If you are going to partner with the Universe, the Divine Mind is going to prompt you to take actions. It's only actions that determine whether you are serious or not. Your true beliefs always show up in the actions that you are willing to take.

When I was a personal trainer, the number one reason that people came to me for, was to lose weight. In the initial consultation, I could pretty much tell if they were going to be successful in losing weight or not. All my weight loss clients said that they wanted to, but their actions proved otherwise. When you truly want to change, trust me, the Universe gets behind you and gives you the tools you need to change. It won't always be easy, and there will be times when you feel like throwing in the towel. However, if you keep turning within to where the true Source of your power lies, and follow the directions coming from Your Other Self, I believe that there is nothing you can't achieve.

However, if you don't really want whatever it is you *say* you want, well, the Presence within you knows that, and will give you your true desires! I would see this time and again with my clients. They would tell me that they wanted to lose weight, but many of them secretly didn't want to. They enjoyed indulging in over eating and drinking, and didn't really want to eat healthy food in the right portions for their body type.

I remember talking to one person in particular about this. They were telling me how they were struggling with cutting back, when I mentioned that there was a better way. I proposed that they changed what they were asking for. Instead of asking Divine Mind to be thin, to instead ask and believe that they would only desire to eat good, healthy food that was in the right proportion for their body, and that they would *enjoy* that. That way they would naturally shrink down to a healthy weight. It makes sense right? When you only eat what your body needs, and love eating that way, it's not hard, it's easy!

Their response was all too telling.

"But I don't want to do *that*. I want to eat as much as I want and still be thin!"

I tried to press the issue…

"But suppose you actually *hated* to over eat. What if it made you feel awful, and you loved eating the right portions to stay slender, and desired wonderful healthy foods, and it was your delight?"

"I don't want that!" was the reply.

Their words, beliefs and actions showed what they truly wanted, and that was the food. Deep down inside, they didn't really want to be the slender version of themselves. They wanted the extra food.

Before judging this person, if we are honest with ourselves each one of us have done the same thing in some area of our lives. We say we want something, but our actions prove otherwise. You can't fool the Universe. It will always give you what you truly desire. However if you really want to change your beliefs, that's when the magic starts happening! Just like our tree example. You need to not only have the right tree (the inside beliefs) you have to actually plant it (actions). The two go hand in hand.

I have learned this lesson in my own life. Starting out on this journey of partnering with the Universe, I was told that in order to be rich, I needed to feel rich. I was told to go to "rich" places in my town, and go to fancy shops and restaurants. Maybe even go and test drive a car that I would one day want to own. I don't know about you, but when I tried this piece of advice, it left me feeling far from rich. In fact, it only seemed to point out the huge gap of where I was now, to where society told me I needed to be in order to feel happy, and fulfilled, and that I had 'made it.'

I believe that I have a way that works far better for me that I would like to share with you. This method makes me feel prosperous and content now, in THIS PRESENT MOMENT. This system isn't a "fake it to you make it," or "act as if" philosophy. No! This way is simple, as it starts with what you have RIGHT NOW! You see, we often don't even stop to think that all the things we currently have in our lives, our car, clothing, friendships, etc, are all things that once upon a time, didn't exist in our lives! However, you manifested them!

I found that when I started to focus on all the things that I already currently have, my power and gratitude seemed to grow. It's like having a dollar, and investing that. Then having another dollar and investing that. Start investing what you have! When you start investing and focusing on what you have, those very things becoming the building blocks to your future. Get your eyes off others and what society tells you. Instead focus on all the good in your life, and trust me, more good will start showing up!

I found for me that when I think about all the clothes I own, the car I drive, my home, my family and friends, and treat those things like I have just obtained them, in this present moment, my mind starts to process things in a whole different way. I start to feel incredible gratitude to God, and joy starts to well up in me, as I realize how very wealthy I truly am. Don't despise what you have. Don't despise the day of the small beginnings, and definitely don't compare yourself to anyone else. This is *your* unique life experience. You are the star of the show. You can partner with God and the Universe and allow those things that you currently have to be "seeds" for greater things to come.

I'm excited to share with you some of these concepts in more detail in the pages ahead. You will feel carefree and so full of joy NOW! Rather than having to wait until you get that thing or desired outcome to feel happy, we are going to be learning how you can tap into the Source of joy right now.

After all, the reason that we want certain things, is because we believe that they will give us a certain feeling right? We are going to be talking about how to tune into that feeling that you want in THIS PRESENT MOMENT! It's Not About Working For It. It's A Gift.

The whole message of Christ was that you don't have to work by "the sweat of your brow" to make God and the Universe "do stuff for you". It's a gift. It's your birthright. Imagine that it's your wedding day. You and your fiance go to the store and set up a registry of all the things that you would like and need for your new home together. On your wedding day all the guests arrive with beautifully wrapped gifts for the bride and groom. During the reception line though, each guest starts giving you the bill for each of the gifts. You realize that to pay off all the "gifts" that have been purchased, you are going to have to do a lot of extra work in order to pay off the debt. I doubt you would enjoy the rest of the wedding or honeymoon realizing that you were now in the hole for thousands of dollars!

Isn't that what we are like? We think that we have to somehow work and make things happen by our own cleverness, rather than relying on the Divine Mind to give us favor. Now I'm not saying that we should never go to work, but, I am talking about not striving. I have planned a wedding before with my daughter, and while it was a lot of work, it was a labor of love. We loved planning her perfect day together. It wasn't striving. It was a joy. This is what it's like when you partner with the universe. You have the mind/consciousness of Christ within you, guiding you and directing you. It should not seem like work. Things may be challenging sometimes, but when you plug into the Infinite Wisdom that lives inside of you, you will always know what to do. If you are feeling overwhelmed and stressed, chances are you are trying to solve problems and run your life using your own limited human intellect alone.

You have been given THIS PRESENT MOMENT to create what you want right now! What are you waiting for? You have access to the same power that arranged the stars in the night sky!

I don't want this to be just another book that you pick up and think "that's nice." I want you to start applying the principles that we are going to be talking about in the pages ahead. As you do this, that is when you are going to start to see real change in your life. So many times we can get bogged down with trying to make changes in our lives. That is why I'm going to keep coaching you to come back to this PRESENT MOMENT in time. This moment is the only moment in time that you can change your future. To make a permanent change, you are going to have to start living the things we are going to be talking about, one moment at a time.

Be prepared for different things to jump off the page. When those things happen, I believe the Universe is trying to communicate something that you need to know right now. Pay attention. Only you know what that means to you. I believe that when your intuition starts kicking about something, it will not only alter how you might be thinking about something, ie, your beliefs, it will also have a corresponding action.

For example, you can have the belief that you want to lose some weight, but unless you follow through with a definite plan of action, you will never lose those extra pounds.

However, when you partner with the Divine Mind of the Universe, you will have all the favor, wisdom and fortitude to bring those dreams that are deposited into you, to life!

Are you ready?

The time for change is NOW!

CHAPTER ONE

THE PROMISE OF THE PRESENT MOMENT

Do you know that right where you are is where you are meant to be? Every single action of your past has brought you to this present moment, and let me tell you a secret...this present moment holds the seed for your highest good.

Let me explain. I have met people that no

matter what happens, wherever they are, whatever they do, it's never good enough. They always feel that being somewhere else is going to be better than where they are right now. The 'magic elixir' that they are seeking is always in the next person, place or thing.

I knew of someone who was always saying how nasty the town that we live in is. That people are unfriendly, and there is no opportunity and it's just an awful place to live. This is despite the fact that the little beach town has been voted as one of the most beautiful places to live in America, with the number one beach in the U.S! This particular person decided to travel and for a while, each place they would go to would be amazing. They would say how wonderful everything was, so much better than the place they were at previously. However, before long, the complaining would set in again about how ghastly everyone was, and how where they were before was so much better.

I've seen this happen time and time again with people over different things. I remember a woman I knew, said it was impossible for her to get into shape because she didn't have a swimming pool. She finally got a house with a pool. Is she in shape? No, and she's lived in that house with the pool for over ten years now!

We can keep running to the next thing, but

really all that we could ever need can be found in THIS PRESENT MOMENT, because the power to generate the feeling that we are looking for is already within us. You don't need any person, place or thing to make it happen for you. When you truly start to embrace this truth, the freedom that you will experience will be second to none!

Christ talked about this when he was asked about where is the right place to worship. He told the Samaritan woman that was asking him this question, that first of all, God is not some "man in the sky," but pure Spirit, and it wasn't about a particular location, it was about finding that place of spirit and truth.

You do not need to go to some special place

to experience the Presence of God. All you need is already within you. Your very body is a dwelling place for the Divine Mind. A temple of the Spirit. The very same Consciousness that is behind all that you see in the physical world lives in you. Now, I can't prove this to you, but you can experience it for yourself. It's all about becoming aware of your thoughts, and knowing that the Presence within you that is observing those thoughts, your spirit/energy is connected with Infinite Intelligence, AKA God.

Stop waiting for the right time. Your human ego will always make up excuses as to why it's not the right time.
"When I'm in shape, I'll do that."

"When I have more money, I'll start my business."

"When I feel like I'm a better writer, I'll start writing that book."

"When the kids are back are school…"

The list goes on…

I believe that the reason why our ego likes to keep us out of the present moment, is because the moment our full attention is on the present, the ego disappears like fog when the sun comes out. Living in the present is your superpower. It's only in the present that you can start shaping what is to come.

Wherever you are, whatever age you are, whoever you are, if you have a dream in your heart, now is the time to start fulfilling it. You are in the perfect place to start! All you need is already at your fingertips. The ingredients are already there to start constructing that thing that you want to partner with the Universe with, to bring into existence.

Just like Christ said, you don't need to go somewhere special. That Universal Spirit is EVERYWHERE, and is longing to partner with you, and express through you. That is why you were put on this planet! If you do need to be at a particular location, (like the story of me and my husband meeting) you won't have to strive to make it happen. It will happen naturally as you start from where you are NOW!

There is literally no place on earth whether

it's Sedona, Jerusalem, Meca, Tibet, or whatever place may be deemed special or holy, where you can access more of the Divine Mind than where you are right NOW! The only thing that is limiting your access is your own consciousness.

There is an ancient story in the book of Genesis, of a man called Jacob who fell asleep as he was on the road, traveling between towns. While he slept, he had a vision of a staircase, or ladder descending out of the heavens and divine messengers going up and down on the staircase. What is surprising is that when he woke up he exclaimed that God was in that place all along, and he didn't know it!
Just like with Jacob, I would like to put

forward to you that the Divine Mind is right where you are, right now. You just have to "wake up" to that fact and allow it to dawn in your consciousness.

Imagine If

Let's play a game. Just suppose for a moment that you started to think like the most successful business person in the world. The most genius entrepreneur. Let's pretend that your consciousness was the same as theirs.

Or, what about the fittest person you know? What if you suddenly started thinking their thoughts and having their same consciousness? Do you think it would affect your actions and the choices that you made in food and exercise? You bet it would!

You see, the whole key to change in life is your consciousness. I can remember talking with someone close to me about some of the dreams that I had in my heart, and how I would like to write etc. They interrupted me and said something like,
"You'll never be able to do that, that is just not who you are."
Now in times past, I would have agreed with them, but that particular day, something inside of me shifted. While I didn't verbalize what was going on inside, I thought to myself,
"Well, then I will just have to become someone else."
It's not that I didn't like who I was, but I

realized that if I was going to follow my dreams, I had to become a different version of me. The version of me that was able to complete the tasks that I would need to do to accomplish my dreams, and have the fortitude to keep going when things got tough!

Each one of us have different versions of ourselves. Being in the world of fitness for so long, I got to see many different versions of people's bodies. I would watch how people would change from being overweight, unhealthy and out of shape, to fit, toned and full of vibrant health. They were still in essence the same people, but they had changed their consciousness, and as a result their outside appearance and health had changed dramatically too.

The secret to this long term, is not trying to go this alone. Your human intellect, while formidable, is no match for the power of the Divine Mind. When you start to partner with the Universe to make changes in your life, nothing will be able to stop you. Jesus Christ partnered with the Source of Everything all the time. In fact, he said that he didn't do anything unless he saw "the Father" do it. He even said that the words he spoke, and the how he was to say them, he got from Divine guidance. He tuned in his consciousness to the Source of all.

The more we rely on our own human intellect, the less we have the opportunity to partner with the Universe and allow the wisdom of the ages to flow to us with the right answer. We are not meant to face life alone. You are not just your human mind. You are pure consciousness.

Remember now, God is not a man in the sky. We are talking about Infinite Spirit here, Universal Presence and Intelligence. Our human understanding may be finite, but Infinite Intelligence is just that...infinite. You can cast any burden on the presence of God within you, and allow that Presence to help you out in whatever situation you may be up against.

I'm sure that we have all experienced this at some time or another. For example, have you ever tried to remember a particular name, or song, only to have it allude you. When you let it go, your subconscious will go into your memory banks and pull out the information when you are least expecting it, and you will suddenly remember!

I found myself for a few years constantly saying things like,
"I'll never lose the excess weight." And...
"I don't know what to do."

One day, I was meditating and I felt a strong direction to stop saying these things. When we get that hunch, most likely, that is your intuition kicking, and it's always best to listen to it. I might not know what to do in my own human understanding, but the

Universe always knows exactly what to do, and we can lean heavily upon the wisdom of God within to lead the way.

I remember getting a huge unexpected tax bill at the end of the year a few years back, that got me worried about how I was going to pay it. I had picked up my tax return from my accountant, and went white when I saw how much I owed! I sat there in my office, and with each passing minute I found myself sinking lower and lower into despair, as I could not figure out how I was going to pay this unexpected 'burden.'

I suddenly realized that sitting there was not going to help anything, but I felt almost paralyzed with stress and worry. Somehow, I pulled myself out of my stupor, and decided to go for a walk around my neighborhood. I remembered the scripture about casting the burden on the presence of God, and decided that I was going to do just that. Florence Scovel Shinn, one of my favorite authors had talked about using an affirmation to help with this, so I decided to try it out for myself. All this worry was too much for my own human mind to handle. As I walked I said to myself,

"I cast this burden on the Christ within, and I go free."
"I cast this burden on the Christ within, and I go free."
I must have said this over a hundred times as I walked, muttering to myself. I'm sure if

any of my neighbors had seen me, they would have thought that I was delusional!

However, as I was walking and saying this to myself, something strange started to happen. It was like a Presence started to dawn in my consciousness, and the fear and worry that was there, started to be replaced with a peace and tranquility. It was like magic! I don't quite know how the tax bill was paid, but somehow we found the money. The most important thing that I had found though, was peace and a newfound awareness of that amazing Presence that was lying dormant in me the whole time.

Then next time that you have something that seems too big for you to handle, cast it onto the Presence of the Divine Mind that lives inside of you. You can even try it out on everyday situations like direction for the day, finding car keys or whatever else you need.

Why not partner with the Source of Infinite Intelligence on ALL subjects? You will be glad you did!

CHAPTER TWO

HOW TO FLY HIGH IN LIFE

You were born to fly high in life. Each one of us has dreams and aspirations that if followed will cause you to have to leave behind the land of familiarity and discover new horizons. However many of us choose to stay stuck in the proverbial chicken coop so to speak, with our eyes and head looking downward at what is familiar. We never leave the confines of our comfort zone.

I understand that. It is so easy to stay where you are because it's so darn...comfortable. We don't want to change many times because we see that change will bring new problems that we don't know how to deal with. However, when we start acting in THIS PRESENT MOMENT and facing those things that we know how to deal with right now, we can start to become more confident in branching out and expanding our horizons.

Dealing with Challenges and Difficult Situations

In times past and still sometimes today, I can allow difficult situations to get the best of me. My dear husband pointed out to me that I was allowing myself to become too emotionally invested when challenging circumstances would come my way...and let me tell you this. When you want to start moving out of your comfort zone and pursue those dreams inside of you, you will be challenged. Why do you think they call it a comfort zone? It's because it's comfortable!

However is that what you truly want for your life? To live a life where you are never challenged to become the best version of you? What if your kids never wanted to stop wearing diapers, or leave home? We would know that for a normal, healthy adult, there is something very wrong.

A secret that I want to share with you about overcoming challenges and problems in your life has to do with your emotions. You see emotions are simply energy in motion. The more energy or focus you give a particular problem or situation in your life, the bigger that thing is going to become.

I'm sure we have all experienced situations that we can see this come into play. Your boss at the office looks at you funny as you leave on a Friday night. You try to shrug it off, but you keep directing your attention back to that look. The more you think about 'that look' the more attention you give it and the more your energy is directed to that. Remember, your emotions are simply energy in motion. Before you know it, your emotions are literally running away with you. You had heard a few weeks ago that they might be cutting back on staff at your work, and now you just KNOW that the reason your boss gave you a strange look, was because you are going to be let go. Little did you realize that the real reason was that they didn't feel well, and wanted to get out of the office as fast as possible!

What has happened here? You have given a harmless situation an emotional charge that set you into a tailspin and ruined your weekend with worry for something that wasn't even true! This is what many people do all the time. They allow their emotions, their energy in motion to be expended on futile things. This precious energy could be used instead to move forward with their life goals. Each one of us only has a certain amount of energy in any given moment. Why not take that energy and direct it in the direction that you want it to go?

Many times, even if the worst case scenario happens, is it really that bad? What if you do lose your job? What if people laugh at you when you go after your dreams? What if you fail? At the end of the day, many of the things that we think are so bad, really aren't catastrophic. We are simply allowing our minds to run us rather than our true selves, which is our consciousness.

If you put your focus on the good only, no matter what happens, things can be turned around for your good. This is not to negate that bad things happen in life. They do.

However, how we choose to direct our energy toward that situation is going to determine our future.

Here is a simple 3 step process I use when I find myself worrying about things and feel challenged.

ONE
Realize that the more you think about the problem, the bigger it is going to get as you are directing more and more energy toward it, only exacerbating the problem.

TWO
Let go and turn the problem over to the Universe/God. Use the affirmation given in the previous chapter. "I cast this problem on

the Presence/Christ within, and I go free."
Trust that you do not have to face the
situation alone. You can partner with the
Universe and allow God/the Divine Mind to
show you what to do at the right time.

THREE

Choose to start directing all your focus and
attention toward all the good in your life.
Start focusing on the blessings you have.
Your clothes, good food, family, friends,
pets. Anything that makes you feel good. As
you do this you start building up good
energy all around you. Every time you begin
to sense that your mind is trying to draw you
back into thinking about the negative
thing/problem, start speaking out loud about
all the good in your life. This is a sure fire

way to magnify good energy around you. Words are containers that 'hold' whatever you are putting in them.

I have found that this works wonders in my life. The more emotional charge you give to something the bigger it's going to get, and this can work for or against you. The key here is to make it work for you. I cannot stress enough the importance of taking hold of the situation and using your spoken words to help mold the energy around you.

In the book of James in the New Testament, the author talks about how we are like a ship, and the thing that controls where the ship sails is the rudder. The rudder in our case is our tongue. We can think thoughts, and that is powerful, but when we say them we take them out of our head, and project them into the air around us. You actually cause the air molecules around you to vibrate as you speak. Use this tool to help you discharge any negative emotions/energy that are causing you to stay bound in your comfort zone.

I can remember dealing with a situation years ago at a workplace. My husband and I worked there together, and it seemed that from the get go there were always a couple of people there who wanted to see our demise. I can actually remember thinking during one of the group interviews with the board before we were even hired, that a particular individual had already decided they didn't like us, and we hadn't even said or done anything!

It didn't matter what we did, what we changed or how we acted, nothing that we did was right. I was stumped. I remember crying out for higher wisdom, thinking that surely I could win these people over and somehow make them happy. There must be something wrong that *we* were doing.
This went on for a long time, years in fact. We would have reprieves here and there with both my husband and I trying everything in our power to fit the mold that these people wanted. It seemed that the more that we tried, the worse it got. I can remember crying myself to sleep night after night. I was a wreck. I knew that they were

saying all sorts of unkind and untrue things about us behind our back and spreading gossip. I started to find myself becoming withdrawn, and a shell of the happy person I used to be. People started to notice that I had lost my spark. I was becoming more and more miserable.

One day, out of the blue, I realized that I was focusing all my energy and attention on a problem that could never be fixed. It was like a lightning bolt hit me and the Presence within showed me clearly how to deal with what was going on. We were supposed to leave. We had outgrown where we currently were and it was time to move on. I had given away my power to people who did not deserve to wield it over me.

It was like a peace flooded my soul when the the Divine Mind showed me that. These people were simply tools to get us where we were supposed to go next! We went through a lot of heartache leaving that workplace, as it was a ministry working with students that we both loved dearly. However, I can honestly say that looking back, I wouldn't have traded it for what I am now walking in.

Sometimes when you partner with the Universe, things might get uncomfortable and downright painful at times, but when you get through to the other side, the rewards are amazing. I realize that the Source that created me was trying to bring me into greater alignment with my life purpose and staying where I was, was detrimental to that. I didn't want to get out of my comfort zone, but because I was willing to listen to Higher Intelligence and not my own ego, I was finally able to realize what was going on.

Now I'm not saying that this will always be easy, but the end result will be well worth it. It's just like going to the gym. Lifting weights is not difficult, but it's not easy to be consistent enough to see the results you want. When it comes to leaving your comfort zone and heading into new adventures, you will go through challenging times. However, you are not alone. The Source that you came from will guide and direct, and give you all the strength that you need in order to help you deal with each moment as it comes. If you are feeling pressure in a certain situation right now, it could very well be, that you are staying in a place that is too small for you, and it's time to move on.

Just a side note, when I let go of these people, it's like all the power they had over me just dropped. I could see the situation for what it really was. All the little power struggles and games looked so stupid and childish, like middle school drama. However, because I was holding on so tightly, it all seemed grander than it really was. When I let go, and listened to Infinite Intelligence, all their power over me fell like a house of cards.

Now, I'm not saying that when you go

through a difficult time, you have to leave. Each situation is different. That is where you need to tune into the frequency of the Universe and allow yourself to be led by Infinite Intelligence, rather than your own personal intellect alone.

Learning Lessons

When we go through trying times, something that I have learned is that they are leading us to greater revelations about *ourselves.* Many times we do not want to think anything that we deem negative about ourselves, or on the opposite spectrum we are too harsh and only think negatively about ourselves. The key is balance. We need to have an honest evaluation of who we are, so we can strengthen our positive traits and minimize our negative ones.

When you partner with the Universe, you are going to find that the magnificent creator behind what we can see, will start to mold you into the very best version of you that you can be. When you start paying attention to the voice in your head rather than just accepting whatever is going in, you will be amazed at how you have your own personal advisor that can help you with any situation.

From my personal experience I have noticed two aspects when your Inner Wisdom is trying to get your attention.

ONE
It will be positive and uplifting. Now I'm

not saying that Infinite Intelligence will never correct your course, but I have found that it won't be derogatory. I have found that when I spend time reflecting on my life, I can turn inward to where this Presence lives, and allow any actions I may have taken to come into light. Sometimes we make decisions that are not the best, or downright wrong. Being unkind, rude, etc is not part of our higher nature. When you allow yourself to evaluate your actions, you can then adjust and change. When any mistakes come into light, you should not feel worse. Instead they are highlighted so you can make appropriate changes, and can go on to become a better version of yourself. It's all about your *journey.*

TWO

It should be specific. When intuition sparks inside of you, it often comes as a flash. It's not general, but it could either be a clear direction or feeling that you should take a specific action.

When we learn to start trusting the Divine Mind, even good things can come out of what we perceive as bad situations. When we hold onto things and try and obtain a particular outcome, many times we sabotage what the Universe is trying to bring out.

In the example above, I wanted the people I was working with to like us. That was my desired outcome. However, looking back I realize that the whole situation taught me about learning to like myself, regardless of what a human thought about me. It all seems rather silly that I put so much stock in their opinion of me! When I let go of that, things became clear and peaceful!

I walked away from that situation realizing that the most important partnership I would ever experience, was the partnership I had with the Universe, and nothing I could do would cause that power to leave my life.

That holds true for each one of us. The situations that happen in your life can propel to you greater heights. It's all a matter of allowing yourself to see things from the perspective of the Divine.

CHAPTER THREE

HOW TO HEAR 'THE SOURCE' SPEAK

There is a quote from Jesus Christ, where he says that his 'Father' is always working. It is interesting because it tells us something about the Divine Mind, and that is this: there is never a time when you are not able to be consciously connected and allow that Intelligence and wisdom to flow to you. It's always flowing!

I don't believe that the Source has favorites. Many early mystics emphatically stated that the Source of All doesn't play that game. Each person has their own vibrant relationship, and each one of us comes to understand that relationship in a different way.

The situation that I described in the last chapter was a time of deep depression for me. When we left that particular job, we ended up losing most of our friends and my sense of identity that I had built up around that job. I remember wondering where God was in all of this. I felt lost and alone.

Before we left, I felt a little voice inside say to me, "You can have all this (money, security, friendships etc) or obscurity with me." I remember quickly replying,

"Obscurity with you!" I had no idea the amount of change in my heart that would bring.

I expected the Divine Mind to swoop down and change my life for the better, in ways that I deemed right! This is something that when you come into partnership, you have to let go. You have to trust that the Source of all knows the best route for you to take. You have to first *become* the person that is able to bring about your future.

What I realize now, is that I was never alone the whole time. When you feel super happy and on top of the world, don't think for an instant that you are somehow more connected than when you feel unhappy or stressed etc. You are always connected. The difference is your perception!

So how do you start to become more aware of the signs that the Universe is guiding you? Well I'm so glad that you asked, because I'm about to tell you!

I have found that the first step is simply believing that you already have access to the Divine Mind of God. You are already connected, fully. You don't have to get the Universe to do anything! You are always "in", because Universal Intelligence lives within you, and you can never be more connected as you are here and now!
I can remember when I first started to tap into this inner Source of wisdom. It was the

early 90's and I was living in Tucson Arizona at the time. My husband and I were newly married, and he was enrolled at the University of Arizona. He would cycle from our home, to the campus each day. At this time hardly anyone had a cell phone.

He would always be back at about the same time, so when he wasn't home at the normal time one day, I started to become worried. If he was late he would always call me from a pay phone or something. My mind, as mind's tend to do, started to immediately worry that he had been hurt, and maybe got into an accident with a vehicle as he was cycling home.

I could feel anxiety starting to tighten it's

vice like grip on my mind, but for some reason, I decided to do something different that day. Call it a Divine Intervention, but rather than go into full out anxiety/panic mode, I decided to go within to the Source and ask for guidance.

I remember getting a flash of intuition that he was ok and would be home at 4:30pm. Right around 4:30 pm, I heard the scrunching sound of the tires of his bike on our gravel driveway. Apparently he had a flat tire, and didn't have any money on him for a pay phone. He instead asked that I would be told that he would be home at around 4:30pm so I wouldn't worry!

Yours For The Taking

You are a child of the Universe. You are meant to be here at this period of time, and because of that, I can say that all the resources of the Universe are there for you!

You are meant to be here. Just like an orange tree produces oranges, because it wants those oranges to grow, the Universe wants you here. You were put here to blossom and grow, and produce fruit. The Divine Mind wants you here, and you can access all that Mind offers: love, joy, peace, prosperity, abundance...the list goes on.

However, if you don't believe it's yours for the taking, you might be like the passenger on the cruise ship that I once heard a story about...

Once upon a time, a man wanted to travel from Europe to America. He had scrimped and saved in order to purchase the passage to his new life in the land of the free.

The day came when he boarded the ship, but he only had just enough money left to buy some cheese and crackers for the journey across the Atlantic.

He would wistfully watch the other passengers eat a bountiful breakfast, fresh fruit and muffins, bacon, eggs, fresh brewed coffee followed by a lunch fit for a king. Dinner was almost unbearable for him to watch! The delicious smells wafting from the dining room would make him salivate! He would peer through the window like a drooling puppy, watching his fellow passengers feast on fillet mignon, salmon, crispy salads, exotic dishes, followed by sumptuous desserts. After days of eating just dry crackers and cheese, and washing it down with water, the thought of one more cracker was almost unpalatable!

Toward the end of the journey, a fellow passenger approached him and asked him why he never joined the rest of them in the dining hall. Embarrassed, he explained that he only had enough money for the fare, but he was grateful that he was going to start his new life in America.
"Why my dear fellow!" The fellow passenger exclaimed. "Didn't you realize that when you boarded the ship, your fare

included entrance to the dining hall? You could have been feasting with us all along!"

When you came into this world, included with your passage was your entrance to the "Divine Dining Room." You need to just come to the realization of that! The Universe always wants to communicate with you.

If you don't change your view in this and just simply start believing, and have the faith of a child that Jesus Christ talked about, you will never be able to perceive the nudges and synchronicities that the Divine Mind is orchestrating for just you!

I like to think about it this way: the Universe is like an interactive, holographic playground and the Divine Mind or Source of this playground is like your own personal tour guide. Trust that Intelligence to lead you through this incredible experience called life.

Don't allow your mind or personal ego to get in the way and tell you that you don't have access to this incredible Source. You do! That Source resides within you! Start having a little faith, and watch to see how extraordinary 'coincidences' start happening in your life.

CHAPTER FOUR

HOW TO KNOW IF WHAT YOU ARE LISTENING TO IS HARMFUL OR HELPFUL

I confess, I'm not a born optimist. If you too don't always see the sunny side of life, take heart, there is hope for you! Let me ask you a question. If you see you have a voicemail or someone says that they want to talk to you about something, do you generally think

it's going to be something positive or negative? For years I would just assume that anytime somebody said they wanted to talk to me, it would be something negative. This would happen continually, even if there was nothing 'wrong' going on!
My mind had been conditioned to simply think the worst!

I grew up thinking that it was smart *not* to expect the best. That way, you wouldn't be disappointed if whatever you wanted to happen, didn't! Unfortunately, the only thing that did for me was make me very negative. I would wake up first thing in the morning, feeling that most likely something bad would happen that day in some form or another. It was quite a depressing way to live. I remember feeling rather bleak from the moment I opened my eyes.

I first came to understand how negative I was, after reading Norman Vincent Peale's classic, *The Power Of Positive Thinking*. It woke me up to the fact that I could actually choose my thoughts, and that thinking negatively about a situation didn't help negative situations at all! If anything, they only made them worse!

If you continually have negative thoughts running through your mind, it's going to be very difficult to actually feel good. I would say that it's almost next to impossible! The good news though, is that with God, all things are possible, and that the Divine

Presence lives within you!

Think for a moment.

Do you honestly believe that the Infinite Intelligence that created galaxies and stars and all the wonders of the planet we live on, is depressed and negative? That this Genius is always expecting things to turn out badly? When I started to realize, like the mystics of old, that the same power and presence lived in me, an interesting thought came to mind.

What does the Divine Mind think about?

Think about *that* for a moment. What if you could allow that power and presence to flow through *you*? What thoughts would you think about then? My hunch is that you would not be entertaining negative, pessimistic and gloomy ones! Meditate on that, and really let that sink in. If Infinite Intelligence, the Divine Presence was encased in a human body, and put in an amazing holographic Universe to explore and play, what thoughts would that Presence think? The truth of the matter is that the Divine Presence is encased in a human body - yours! Allow that Presence to break through the filter of your mind and illuminate any dark and gloomy thoughts with thoughts of light, peace and joy!

The more you entertain positive and uplifting thoughts, the more connected you will become with the Presence within, and the more you will see the Universe around you corresponding to your new positive vibe!

Now when I say this, I do not mean that nothing 'negative' will ever happen. What I am saying is that you will be able to see beyond just the outer happenstance and perceive it from a whole different level of consciousness.

What do you see?

How we see our life is so vital to what we experience. Do you see life as a war zone, a jungle, a maze, a playground? When I started to realize that my expectations of things actually contributed to how I experienced them, I started to consciously make a shift in my thinking.

I came to the place of understanding that one of the most profound things I could do with my life, was to raise my consciousness. I wanted to have a good vibe, and I started to see that the more I had a good vibration going on, the more I was connected and partnered with the Universe.

Start small. Start believing that the Divine Presence within you wants you to think good thoughts. Why would that Presence want to think destructive and pessimistic things? A simple way to start this process, is to consciously start to think about all the things that make you feel good, that is, all the things that you are thankful for.

So many times we are focused on what we don't have, rather than what we do. When we start to think about our clothes, home, pets, food, friends etc, it starts to open the channel for the Presence within to start to connect with the Universe outside!

The Bridge
Inside of you dwells the Presence of God, which wants to partner, so to speak with this amazing holographic world that you are in. The whole created Universe is like a thought in the Mind of the Infinite. The Bridge between the two worlds is *your* mind. Think of the Presence within you like a breathtaking castle where the Sovereign

ruler lives. All around the castle is a moat, when the draw bridge is down, it enables the King or Queen to visit the Universe without. Your mind or personal ego is like that drawbridge. When you lay it down, the true Presence within can truly 'explore' the Universe without. This is what Jesus Christ meant when he said that you have to lay down your life in order to find true life.

The Key to manifesting things is to bring the personal ego into alignment with the will of the Presence within you. Your personal self has no clue whether something might be detrimental to you or not, and cannot see the larger picture. When people get discouraged that something that they want is not coming to pass, it could be that something even better is coming their way! If your name is on the Divine Title, it's yours, and nothing can take it away from you! Your True Self, is in partnership with the Universe, and when the two come together, well that's when miracles happen!

CHAPTER FIVE

HOW TO NOTICE WHEN YOU ARE IN PARTNERSHIP WITH THE UNIVERSE

As I talked about in a previous chapter, the Divine Mind within you is not depressed, anxious, worried or generally unhappy. To start having more of the emotions that you want in your life, start noticing and paying attention to the things in your life that make you feel good, joyful, and at peace. As you do this, you will notice how you seem to attract more and more things that make you feel good, joyful, at peace and happy!

Let me give you an example. A few years ago, I bought a Black Mustang GT. I knew that Mustang's were pretty popular cars, but it wasn't until I was driving mine, that I noticed how many were on the road! They were everywhere! It seemed that I was always pulling up next to one, behind one, or they were next to me when I parked. Why? Because my mind had now been conditioned to look for Mustangs.

If you are struggling with gloomy thoughts, most likely your mind has been conditioned to entertain those thoughts. All of us have thoughts that lower our vibration and can bring us down. However, it's our choice whether we want to entertain them or not.

Think about your TV set. No doubt you have randomly flipped through the channels looking for something to entertain you. When something seems interesting, you stay on the channel, or frequency, and the show or movie starts to come alive before your eyes. It's up to you to decide what you want your mind to entertain itself with.

You are holding the remote, so to speak, and whatever channel you decide to entertain is what is going to show up in *your* Universe. If you want a change in your life, you HAVE TO CHANGE THE CHANNEL!

Did you notice?

A little game that is fun to play is to start noticing a certain thing in your life. For example, because I became conscious of Black Mustangs I started to see them, and other color Mustangs everywhere!
For this little game, pick something that you would like to see more of in your life.

It could be the color blue, or people smiling at you, or a certain animal etc. Whatever it is, just make sure it is something that makes you feel uplifted.

Remember the Presence within you will start to partner with the Universe without, when you are on the same frequency and it will seem like that thing is literally everywhere!

When you start to consciously play "The Notice Game" it's like more and more synchronicities start showing up as well! For example, you fancy a hamburger from your favorite local hamburger joint, and that day when you go to your mailbox, you just happen to get a coupon for half off your favorite burger

You can pass them off and say that they are just coincidences, but when more and more crazy things start showing up, you start to realize that the Universe is partnering up with the Presence inside of you, and it starts showing up in this hologram of life!

Just a couple of years ago, my husband remarked that he had never seen a coyote where we lived in Florida. We had lived in the desert in the Southwest, and coyote sightings were common. However after two decades of living in Florida,we had never seen one! The next day, a coyote passed by right in front of my husband's truck in broad daylight! Coincidence? I think not! We have had too many unexplainable "coincidences" happen over the years to think that situations like these just *happen*! And let me tell you this, it can sure make life a lot more fun and adventurous!

I promise you that when you start opening your eyes to all the wonderful things going on around you, you will feel like you are living right in the middle of a fairytale where anything could happen! Imagine getting up with the expectancy of a child on Christmas morning, knowing that each day is going to be full of wonderful hidden things that you get to spot! It will make everyday, mundane living anything but!

Of course, each one of us have difficult and trying times that we go through, it's part of living on planet earth. However, I've noticed that even in painful situations, when you start allowing a new awareness to your life's events, you will start to see how certain things show up in your life, at just the right time. Or if they didn't, you can look back and see from a later perspective that it was because something better was coming your way.

Start having fun and playing with the

Universe, knowing that it is your natural habitat. You are meant to be here at this time and place, and you can direct your experience by allowing the Presence within you, out, through the bridge of your mind.

CHAPTER SIX

FOLLOWING YOUR INTUITION

Have you ever had a hunch that you were supposed to do something but didn't? Or maybe you felt you were not supposed to do something, but charged ahead anyway only to regret it? We can look back on situations like that and say to ourselves, "I knew I shouldn't have done that!" I can remember feeling rather tired and cranky one evening. Being irritable I was amount to say a remark to my husband when a little voice inside said something like,

"Don't say that, it will lead to an argument. You're grumpy just go to bed."

Did I listen? No! My mind/ego got in the way, and the prediction was right. However, next time the same situation happened, I learned from it, went to sleep, and woke up in a happy state of mind.

That little voice that speaks from within, is none other than Infinite Intelligence, gently nudging us to make decisions that are in our best interest. They might not always be easy, but they will feel right. Intuition simply means, "taught from within." I have made mistakes, but the more I have practiced following my intuition, the more I am able to recognize more clearly if I am partnering with the Universe, or my own mind/ego.

It's wonderful to know that no matter what you are going through in the outside world, there is no problem too big for the Universe and the Presence of the Divine Mind within you. They are an unstoppable force.
When we are facing a difficult situation, what we tend to do is use only the resources available to us from our limited mind memory bank. We worry and fret, because we can't see any possible solution to the situation. We might be confined physically through time and space, but the Universe is vast, and the Presence of Divine Mind/God within you is all knowing and saw the problem coming. You are not alone - ever.

Picture for a moment a ship out at sea. Fishing boats are equipped with fish finders, which use SONAR in order to find fish. It's a similar technology to RADAR . If a captain is out on the ocean fishing and he doesn't see any fish, he doesn't assume that there are no fish out there. He knows beyond a shadow of a doubt that there are fish in that ocean, he just needs to either

1. Wait for them to come to him.

2. Move his ship to where the fish are.

When you are going through a difficult time and can't see any help on the radar, don't for a minute think that it's not there. The Universe has the answer to what you need, and Infinite Intelligence can steer you to where you need to be. Sometimes you might actually be the answer to someone else's problem.

Let me give you an example. I am a very structured person, and like to stick with a routine. It's just my personality. Anyway, just last week I was sitting in my office when I had a strong sense that I should head to the gym. I looked at the time only to realize that it was about three hours before I normally workout, so I carried on doing whatever it was I was doing. However, the feeling wouldn't go away, so after a few minutes, I changed into my gym clothes, and headed out the door.

Halfway through my workout, a young man who I didn't at first recognize approached me and said,

"Would you happen to be so and so's (my son's name) mom?"

"Yes." I replied.

He went on to explain who he was, that he was a friend of my son's and had been away in the military for the past four years, and had wanted to reconnect with him. He was now back in town, and he hadn't been able to reach him as he did not have his new phone number. I suddenly remembered who he was as he had come over multiple times to our home as a teenager. He had long hair in high school, which was now military short! I gave him the new phone number, and when I told my son about it, he had said that just the other day he was wondering how this particular friend was!

Shortly after I got back from the gym, it started to pour torrentially, and didn't let up for the rest of the day! I couldn't help but smile to myself thinking that I got to be a part in reconnecting old friends. If I hadn't gone to the gym when I did, I would've missed my son's friend. Also, I got the added bonus of not being soaked to the skin from the massive thunderstorm, because I had been flexible and gone at a different time from normal.

I share these stories, because the Universe is no respecter of persons. It's a beautiful holographic reality made out of pure energy from the very Presence of the Divine Mind. The very same Presence that is within you. There is only one life in existence, having a multitude of different experiences through all the different personalities that make up this beautiful, exciting and adventurous world we live in.

All around you, each day, are wonderful fantastical stories going on, and you get to be the star of your story! You just have to believe that you have Infinite Intelligence inside of you, partnering with the Universe you see, to create the story of your life. How you direct your story is really up to you by how you choose to perceive things with your mind.

In his little pamphlet, *The Golden Key*, Emmet Fox talks about how the Golden Key to life is simply a shift in your consciousness. Whenever a problem surfaces, rather than putting all your focus and attention on the problem, simply shift your attention to the consciousness within, the Presence of God that dwells inside you. The answer is not going to be found by putting all your attention on the problem, but instead putting all your attention on where the solution to the problem can be found instead!

It may sound overly-simplistic, but it seems that the most profound things in life are. When you get back to that primal energy that is within, and focus upon that, you are going to get a prime answer! It can even help with everyday irritants. For example, I woke up this morning to find that my credit card had been fraudulently charged. I started to feel quite irritated that somebody had the audacity to run up almost $200 on a complete stranger's tab. However, when I turned within to that Primal Presence of the Divine, I felt peace come over me. I simply called the credit card company, took care of it, and moved on. So many times we want to linger on those little irritants that come our way, which rob us of the peace that could be ours!

This would be another great time to use the "cast the burden" technique explained in a previous chapter. Remember the more attention you give a problem, the more it is going to grow in your mind, and turn up in the created, seen world.

It's All Going To Work Out
When you start to believe that things are always going to work out for the best, you can start to feel more at ease. Start intentionally shifting your perspective from what's right in front of you, and instead start seeing yourself as an energetic being, connected with the Divine, and at one with the Universe.

Some years ago when my husband and I were newly married, we got into a little traffic accident. Someone rear ended us, and because we weren't at fault, we received a check for the repair to our back bumper. Before the check came in the mail, we had a freak wind storm come through our neighborhood that did minor roof damage to our home. Shortly after that, we received the check in the mail from the insurance company that we were able to use to fix the roof ! Sometimes when seemingly "bad things" happen, you are being set up for something good! Believe it!

CHAPTER SEVEN

PERFECT PLANNING

Many times our brains try and figure out how things are going to work out. We plot and plan, hoping that we can make things turn out the best way that we think they should. However, we simply can't see the whole picture, but the Universe knows everything that is going on in the world, and will lead you to the best possible outcome when you allow it.

Allowing is the operative word here. Our intellectual minds are only so clever, but the

Presence within, partnered with the Universe without, is an unstoppable force!

It's impossible to predict how things are going to happen! Just thinking back to how I met my husband, there is no way that I could have orchestrated our meeting in Las Vegas. All I knew was that I wanted to find an incredible life partner. Up until that point I had said that I wanted to be with someone who had long rocker type hair (it was the late 1980's and Bon-Jovi hair was big). They also had to drive a sports car! I dated a few people who fit the above description, but it just wasn't "right." When I finally gave up on picking the specifics and instead relinquished the choice of the best person for me, to the Presence of God within me, well along came my husband. He drove a van at the time I met him and he has a shaved head...but let me tell you something, he's perfect for me! We have been together now for thirty years!

I gave up telling the Universe what I wanted and how I thought it should be. Many times we don't know what we truly want. Now I know that this may fly in the face of what you might have heard before, but think about this. If you keep getting things that disappoint you, maybe your desires are not on point with what you *really* want. Our limited intellect only knows so much! I thought I wanted a long-haired rocker type, but the Divine Mind knew what would really fulfill me. That same Presence within you, knows what would really fulfill you too!

You can trust that Infinite Intelligence is way more intelligent than your intellect and will bring to you what is the very best for you, if you allow it! Imagine having the most Intelligent Being helping you in all situations when you don't know what to do. Well let me tell you a secret, that Intelligence that you need, is inside of you!

Focus on the Good

Think of yourself in a car, going to a place that you have never been to before, with no map, phone, or GPS. You would be lost! However if you had a friend that knew the exact location by heart, the easiest thing to do is to let that friend drive! It's the same when you partner with the Universe - just be the passenger, along for the ride, and enjoy the journey!

The key here is to simply focus your attention on the final destination. You might not know exactly where this destination is, but you know it's going to be good! That's where your focus should be. On the good. That is your final destination. You get to choose! Choose the good. Don't worry about the details. Simply focus on the good things, and don't entertain worrying or troubling thoughts, or wonder, "will it work out?" Remember, energy flows where attention goes. Even if you can't see exactly how something might end up, focusing on the good helps bring about a good outcome.

It truly is a shift in your consciousness or perspective that can make all the difference in how your days go. Trust that your Divine Partner knows how to work things out on your behalf, and prepare to be pleasantly surprised!

The One Thing

In this life, there are so many things that seem to press on us. Bills to pay, weight to lose, children to attend to, houses and laundry to keep clean. However, in the midst of all the busy-ness of life, you can always choose to focus on one thing.

Each one of us wants the best for ourselves.

Even when we moan and complain, sometimes we do it, simply because we are addicted to the feeling that it gives us. You could say, "who wants to feel misery?" I'm sure that every day you run into people who have formed the habit of complaining and grumbling about things. It doesn't matter how well things may be going for them, they will always find something to complain about. Over time, they have most likely bought into the habit of complaining, and they don't even realize it! They have become unconsciously addicted to the rush of emotions that complaining gives them.

This can prove to be one of the most difficult habits to break. However the habit or grumbling and complaining about life's circumstances tend to keep us focused on everything that is not good is our lives, so much so that we fail to see all the amazing things around us. While it may be hard, it is not impossible. When you Partner with the Universe, you are better able to see the good in this world. Allow that Presence, Your Other Self to start taking control. When you allow your mind to be infused with Infinite Intelligence rather than your own intellect, you will have a whole other resource at your fingertips.

If you have found that you have inadvertently got yourself into the rut of complaining, ask Infinite Intelligence to give you a gentle nudge every time you start to think a complaining thought and give voice to that. Whatever we give voice to, tends to become more real. As we already talked about, this Universe is a mass of moving energy. When you speak, the sound waves you produce interrupt the energy field around you and can either bring about positive or negative vibrations.

Many people have lived in a negative energy vibration for so long, that living in a positive one, seems to foreign to them. This explains why complainers tend to hang out with complainers, and positive, enthusiastic people tend to hang out with like minded people. As the old saying goes, "birds of a feather, flock together." Put a complainer with someone who is full of joy, and it can be almost unbearably painful to them. The energy is upsetting the frequency they are on.

If you want to know what frequency you are on, take a look at those you hang out with the most. Are they uplifting and encouraging to you? Do they want to encourage you in your dreams and ambitions? Are they honest and have integrity with how they live their lives? It's most likely that they are on a good energy frequency.

However, if your "friends" put you down, complain, gossip about others, are dishonest etc, you have to ask yourself, is that who you want to be too? Because trust me, your vibe really does attract your tribe.

If you want to get out of negativity here is a simple formula I use:

1
2. Ask Infinite Intelligence to give you a nudge every time you think or speak something that is negative and complaining.
3. Ask Infinite Intelligence to give you a more uplifting thought instead.

When you allow your conscious mind to be activated by Infinite Intelligence, that is the power of Your Other Self coming into play. Trust that your energy is changing. Your energy and reality are changing with each moment that passes. Remember, that the only time you can ever change anything is in the PRESENT MOMENT. Change happens in a twinkling of an eye. Each moment is an opportunity for you to be in an entirely new reality. A good reality. Each MOMENT is a chance to begin again. It's up to you to simply accept that fact. It's moments strung together over a period of time that make things seem real to us, more substantial. But, truth be told, each moment has enough substance in itself to create the future you desire.

However, if you keep focused on what you don't want, you are creating that reality over and over again by each moment you choose to focus on that! Let go of the past reality, and trust the Presence within to start manifesting your desired result in the Universe.

CHAPTER EIGHT

YOUR MIND SPACE

Each one of us only has a certain amount of mind space that we can use to occupy thoughts in. It's entirely up to us to choose what occupies that mind space. However, if we allow it to, our runaway minds will fill that mind space up with things that are counterproductive. It's time to take back your mind space!

Let's play a little game here. Let's suppose you wake up one morning and notice that you should properly take your favorite shirt to the dry cleaners so it's ready to wear next time. Imagine now if you thought about your favorite shirt as you showered, drove to work, were at the gym, cooking dinner, brushing your teeth. You couldn't get that darn shirt off your mind no matter what. It started to haunt you. Even though you didn't actually need the shirt or plan to wear it anytime soon, it's all you could think about. Crazy huh? A small thing like a shirt, taking up so much room in your mind!

Well, it's the same way when it comes to other problems that enter into our lives. I bring up the silly example of the shirt because we actually do it all the time. The simple solution would be to take it to the dry cleaners, and stop thinking about it. When it comes to different things that crop up in our life, we spend way too much time thinking about them. We think about it even when the actual thing we are worrying about isn't' effecting us. It's all in our minds.

The problem of the shirt didn't actually really exist, because you didn't need the shirt at that point in time. Many times, we allow things to affect us when the actual physical reality of whatever it is, isn't actually present. For example, if you are dealing with a difficult person at work, you might only interact with that person for less than an hour or so a week. However, it seems so much more, because you are spending so much of your mind space thinking about it. You are inadvertently creating a bigger problem because you are allowing it to take up more space than what it occupies in actual physical reality.

> A little mantra that I like to use is:
> This is my life NOW.

Getting back to what is going on in the PRESENT MOMENT, helps me to keep my focus on what is really going on in my physical reality, and not my mind space. Your mind space is precious, and the more you allow Your Other Self (the part of you that is connected to God) to be in charge of that space, the better you are going to feel and navigate through this world!

Stop giving attention to the "shirts" in

your life. The things that you aren't actually "wearing' or having to deal with in the present moment. When you become aware of how often you are not actually in the present moment, is when you will free up mind space to enjoy the reality you are in RIGHT NOW!

Creating the Future Now

I'm sure that one time or another each one of us has gone through a break up. Whether it's romantic, a friendship or business related, it can be painful. Sure, there is a grieving time in order to process what has happened, but if you want to move on with your life, and not stay stuck in the past, you have to commit to leaving the past behind, and actively creating your future.

I remember a friend giving me advice years ago, that if I wanted to get over a breakup, the best way was to stop dwelling on that person. Sitting around thinking about them, looking at their photo etc, was not conducive for me to move on with my life. I remember realizing that if I wanted to create a new future, I had to start now, and not have things in my life that would remind me of things/people that were no longer supposed to be in my life.

Your energy is currency, an energetic force running through your body. Whatever you pay attention to, you can be sure that you are actually using up your currency. Do you really want to use your precious resources on things that are going to keep you in the past?

As a child, I remember watching a movie adapted from the book *Great Expectations* by Charles Dickens. I was eerily moved by the character of Miss Havisham. She had been jilted on her wedding day by her fiance, and refused to take off her wedding dress. Not only that, she never left her house to see the light of day and stopped all the clocks so that she was stuck perpetually in the past in that moment in time. She remained like that for decades, an old woman, dressed in her wedding dress, with everything around her buried in dust, slowly rotting away. That remained her reality until she died when her wedding dress caught on fire.

I remember getting chills from the bizarre character she played, and wondered how anyone could ever choose a life like that. Truth be told, that many of us choose that life. Like Miss Havisham, we choose to hold on to things that remind us of pain, and we slowly age, never seeing the light of this PRESENT DAY again.

If only Miss Havisham had taken a short time to grieve and reflect on what happened, and then taken off her wedding dress, removed all traces of the wedding banquet around her, and allowed time to move on, she could have experienced love again. Instead she chose to hold onto pain, and recreated the past, day after day until she died.

We don't have to choose a life like Miss Havisham. If you want to move on, get rid of the painful things that hold you back and keep you locked in the painful past. At least put them in a box, out of sight if you can't part with them at the moment. Our outer environment can really affect our inner environment too.

Surround Yourself With Things You Love
Instead of holding onto things from the past that cause you pain, choose to surround yourself with things that make you feel good, things that you would like to see more of in the future. Cleaning up your outside environment so that it is organized and clean, can do wonders for you in the way of your energy level.

I personally find it very difficult to work in a cluttered disorganized space. I tend to be a minimalist, and only want things around me that are either beautiful or useful. Let me share a simple technique I use to keep my outside universe in order

The Twenty Minute Technique

Each day I set aside two twenty minute periods. I set the timer on my phone and for the first twenty minutes I clean and organize our home. I start at one end of the house, and do as much as I can before the timer goes off. By the end of the week, the whole house has been cleaned. Also doing a little every day keeps clutter away. Housework might not be your favorite thing to do, but twenty minutes goes by fast, and when you are consistent with this, before too long your outside world will be organized and that can really help with your inner state.

For the second twenty minutes, again I put my timer on and take care of another household task. It could be folding laundry, paying bills, pulling weeds, doing some extra organizing of a drawer or closet. Once again, when the twenty minutes is done, I'm done.

I discovered this technique years ago when I had small children, and it has served me well. Try it for yourself, and feel free to make any tweaks in it that work better for you.

You might be wondering what this possibly has to do with partnering with the Universe. How I see it, is that the Universe is orderly. There are seasons, Spring, Summer, Autumn and Winter, day and night, high tides and low tides. You can predict nature to be orderly. Just take a walk in the forest, or a deserted beach and you will feel the tranquility around you. You owe it to yourself to make your home a tranquil and peaceful sanctuary.

Your Inner Space

It's important to take care of your mental space too. During the recent Covid-19 pandemic, it seemed like my entire social media feed was mainly made up of fear and panic. What was even more surprising to me, was that my mind strangely wanted to stay connected to it. It was like it wanted the rush from all the drama surrounding it and started to become addicted to it. I'm not advocating being in the dark about important situations going on in the world. Instead, I encourage you to evaluate how much time you are feeding your mind with those things and your perception of those things. Is it all doom and gloom, or do you believe that the Higher Consciousness behind this created world is bigger than finite humanity?

I found myself starting to become more and more anxious and fearful, although I didn't realize it. It was the whole proverbial frog in the kettle. Put a frog in hot water, it's going to immediately jump out. Put a frog in cold water, slowly turn up the heat and it will boil to death.

It suddenly dawned on me one day, that all the fear I had been feeding my mind was causing me to feel less than happy. In fact, I was at the beginning stages of depression and felt disconnected from the Presence of God within. If you are finding that social media is having a negative effect on you, try limiting how much time you give to it. Also if you have friends who insist on posting things which cause you distress, you can simply unfollow their feed. You owe it to your peace of mind. Remember, the ego loves drama, and wants to convince you that you will be missing out if you don't keep up with all the latest gossip. However I believe it's in our best interest instead to cultivate a deeper awareness of the Power within by meditating on the good in this world. When we do that, we start to notice the good showing up more and more in our outer experience.

A Little Smile Goes a Long Way

Just like the example of taking care of household tasks a little at a time, rather than spending hours at the weekend on household chores, you can use that same technique with your state of mind.

If you want to bolster your happiness factor, here's another tip. Set a timer on your phone to go off each hour, and choose to smile. I mean choose to light up the room with those pearly whites. Try and hold it for at least 30 seconds. You will start to feel different when you start to make this a practice. The reason why is that our physicality and our spirituality are intrinsically linked. You can't help but start to feel good when you smile. Believe that the Divine Mind is smiling through you, using your body as an expression in this world, because in reality, that is the truth. It works like magic!

CHAPTER NINE

INFINITE POSSIBILITIES

When you wake up each morning, you are waking up to a field of infinite possibilities, because the Infinite lives in you. When your mind partners that Presence, Your Other Self comes out to play in this beautiful holographic Universe. Life literally becomes an adventure where anything can happen.

Movie Magic

If you are anything like me, I bet you enjoy

a good movie from time to time. One of my favorite movies is Forrest Gump. It's so deep and profound as you watch Forest navigate through life. There are good times and bad. Tragic moments and ones that are so hilarious that they will have you laughing out loud.

What I love about movies is that you can watch objectively as the characters live out their choices on the screen before you. What many of us don't realize is that our own lives are like movies. Each one of us gets to be the leading role in the movie of our lives. A movie is a plethora of still shots strung together to form a moving picture. If you think about it, that is what each one of our lives truly is. Individual moments strung together to produce a feeling of movement or life.

Don't be the cameo or side kick in your movie. You are the starring role, the lead actor, and you can play any part you want. You might think,
"But my life is so dull and boring. Nothing ever exciting happens."

That's what Lucy thought until she entered what looked like an ordinary wardrobe in an English country house, and found herself in the magical country of Narnia.

Narnia, so to speak is all around you. It's about a shift in your perspective. Allow Your Other Self to take center stage, and life will start to become exciting. It's not so much that your outer circumstances change dramatically, although they will start to shift, but it's more your consciousness.

Let me give you an example in my own life. For a few years I owned and operated a cleaning business. I live in a sub-tropical climate and had a few homes that I took care of. Some of these homes were on a small series of islands, just off the mainland. One day as I was driving back, it was like I was suddenly seeing it for the first time. I felt like I had been transported to another world. The balmy tropical air, the gorgeous foliage around me. There were my hands gripping the steering wheel. I was in the driving seat of my life. Each choice I made would have consequences and change the entire course of my life. I felt caught up in a story larger than life! It was exhilarating!

I could turn to the right and choose to go right home, or I could turn to the left and go...anywhere I wanted! I was in awe of the power that was in my hands, and it was all because I woke up to the fact that the Consciousness that made the entire Universe was somehow experiencing the world through me, through my physical body. This was like virtual reality par none!

Your Persona

Each day can be an adventure if you accept that invitation. Your mind or ego would like to keep you locked in set boundaries of who you think you are, but you don't have to remain that if you don't want to. You can grow, you can evolve, you can be anybody you choose to be. By allowing Your Other Self to take charge, the world is at your fingertips. Your joy, your bliss, is not dependent upon what happens in the world around you. What you are looking for can only be found inside.

The only time that you can ever change your life, is in the present, and you can change the whole perception of who you are in a split second. For example, the other day I was visiting a dear friend at her home. Before I left, she handed me a bag, and said, "I ordered these tops, and they just don't fit me right. They are really cute, and I thought that you might like them."

Now my friend is twenty years younger than me, drop dead gorgeous, and probably the most in shape person I have ever met. Besides that she is extremely kind and gracious. It's always hilarious to go out with her to see the looks she gets, and the stares of admiration which she seems oblivious to.

Looking at the tops when I got home, I realized that I would never have ordered them. They were super cute, tasteful, yet sexy - not what I would typically wear! When I tried them on, I felt like a completely different person. I felt amazing! Is this how my friend feels I wondered? My husband said I looked amazing too, and I felt years younger. What had happened? I had simply dressed ***out of character***, and had taken on a different persona. Each one of us dress and act according to a certain part that we feel we should play. If you don't like the character you are playing, you can change it! You can choose to be whoever you want. We each will feel the most at home when we align ourselves with the presence within.

Feeling Is The Secret
The famous Metaphysical teacher Neville Goddard wrote a whole book about how your feelings really are the secret to everything in your life.
Feelings and emotions are different. Emotions are energy in motion in the body. Whatever energy you set in motion will cause certain feelings to be generated. As we

already talked about, wherever you put your attention is when your energy will flow. Put your attention on good things, your energy in motion (your emotions) will cause good feelings to start to come to the surface of your mind.

You can choose what feeling you want to feel by choosing what energy you want to pass through your **body**. When I wore the tops my friend gave me, I had a shift in my energy. You can choose what feeling you want to experience by changing your conscious awareness.

Just like in the smile technique previously mentioned, your physicality can play a big role in your emotional state. If you want to change the persona in the movie of your life, and want to switch up the character you are playing, what would that character do? I always wanted to write and be an author, but guess what, I never wrote! Or, if I did, it was very sporadic. I realized that if I was going to be a writer, I need to do what writers do - write!

I decided that I was going to set my timer for one hour a day and make it a priority to write. As I sit down to write this, I honestly don't know what words are going to come out next. I trust that as My Other Self partners with the Universe, the right words will appear on this screen through my fingers!

What do you want to do? Who do you want to be? Many times we can't immediately jump into the feeling of what character we would want to play. However, when we start using the physicality of our bodies, we can start building a whole new persona. Whatever you want to achieve in life, when you start living in this PRESENT MOMENT, and putting your full awareness there, you can start cultivating whatever character it is that you would like to play. What have you always dreamed of doing? What have you always wanted to be like? The choice is entirely up to you. Don't look to anyone else. Remember you are the star of YOUR movie.

The Miraculous Mundane

The definition of the word "mundane" is:

Lacking interest or excitement, dull, or Of this earthly world rather than a heavenly or spiritual one.

I am sure that we all experience the mundane every day of our lives. However, really it is all an illusion. The reason that I say this, is because we have it all backwards. Rather than being human earthbound creatures trying to have a spiritual or conscious experience, we are actually spiritual beings, encased in this earthly body, having a human experience. That is anything but mundane or boring.

This makes me think of the movie Avatar. The lead character, Jake Sully who is a quadraplegic, finds himself on the planet

Pandora, where he is part of a military experiment. This experiment enables his mind or consciousness to inhabit a body that looks like the native humanoid race of Pandora, a beautiful and wild species called the Na'vi. For the first time in a long time, Jake is able to experience being able to walk and run, but it's more than just the physical sensations of motion that he is able to experience. He is also able to experience reality in a whole new way. He starts to experience it as one of the Na'vi, and falls in love with their whole culture.

When the Divine Mind created your body, placed your consciousness inside of it and put you on planet earth, it was meant to be anything other than boring, dull and lacking excitement. Your whole experience can actually be likened to Jake Sullys. You were sent here to awaken to the Presence of God within you. The Presence of the Divine Mind, partnering with the Universe to experience all that planet earth has to offer.

When you start seeing your life as an amazing adventure where you allow your mind to be connected to the Presence of God within you, you will never be the same again. The beauty of Your Other Self, which is the human personality, entwined with the One Consciousness that permeates the entire created world is that feeling, that energy in motion that you have been looking for your whole life. Nothing outside of yourself can bring you what you are looking for, because it's already inside of you.

The earth realm, the realm of the so-called mundane, is actually the realm of the miraculous. The earth realm is not lacking in excitement, it is the epitome of excitement. Many times we don't realize that we are right smack in the middle of a miraculous event until after the fact. The good old days that you may long for are actually happening right now!

It's time to embrace all you are on the inside, and allow Your Other Self to live the life of your dreams.

It's time to partner with the Universe!

Made in United States
Orlando, FL
16 November 2021